Presented to:

....

From:

....

Date:

....

100
days
of
thanks

THOMAS NELSON
Since 1798

Published in Nashville, Tennessee, by Thomas Nelson. Thomas Nelson is a registered trademark of HarperCollins Christian Publishing, Inc.

Thomas Nelson titles may be purchased in bulk for educational, business, fund-raising, or sales promotional use. For information, please e-mail SpecialMarkets@ThomasNelson.com.

Unless otherwise indicated, Scripture quotations are taken from the Holy Bible, New International Version®, NIV®. Copyright © 1973, 1978, 1984, 2011 by Biblica, Inc.™ Used by permission of Zondervan. All rights reserved worldwide. www.zondervan.com. The "NIV" and "New International Version" are trademarks registered in the United States Patent and Trademark Office by Biblica, Inc.™

Scripture quotations marked CEB are taken from the Common English Bible. Copyright © 2011 Common English Bible.

Scripture quotations marked CEV are taken from the Contemporary English Version. Copyright © 1991, 1992, 1995 by American Bible Society. Used by permission.

Scripture quotations marked ESV are taken from the ESV® Bible (The Holy Bible, English Standard Version®), copyright © 2001 by Crossway, a publishing ministry of Good News Publishers. Used by permission. All rights reserved.

Scripture quotations marked KJV are taken from the Holy Bible, King James Version (public domain).

Scripture quotations marked MSG are taken from *The Message*. Copyright © by Eugene H. Peterson 1993, 1994, 1995, 1996, 2000, 2001, 2002. Used by permission of NavPress. All rights reserved. Represented by Tyndale House Publishers, Inc.

Scripture quotations marked NASB are taken from the New American Standard Bible®. Copyright © 1960, 1962, 1963, 1968, 1971, 1972, 1973, 1975, 1977, 1995 by The Lockman Foundation. Used by permission. (www.Lockman.org)

Scripture quotations marked NCV are taken from the New Century Version®. Copyright © 2005 by Thomas Nelson. Used by permission. All rights reserved.

Scripture quotations marked NKJV are taken from the New King James Version®. Copyright © 1982 by Thomas Nelson. Used by permission. All rights reserved.

Scripture quotations marked NLT are taken from the Holy Bible, New Living Translation. Copyright © 1996, 2004, 2007, 2013, 2015 by Tyndale House Foundation. Used by permission of Tyndale House Publishers, Inc., Carol Stream, Illinois 60188. All rights reserved.

Scripture quotations marked NRSV are taken from the New Revised Standard Version Bible. Copyright © 1989 National Council of the Churches of Christ in the United States of America. Used by permission. All rights reserved.

Scripture quotations marked THE VOICE are taken from The Voice™. Copyright © 2008 by Ecclesia Bible Society. Used by permission. All rights reserved.

Library of Congress Cataloging-in-Publication Data
ISBN 978-1-4003-1113-2

Printed in China
18 19 20 21 HH 5 4 3 2 1

Contents

Introduction

Gratitude is an art—acquired through our observations or life experiences. Though at times it seems a lost art, when we're mindful of how essential the practice is to our well-being, we are eager to include the application of thankfulness to our daily rituals. Scripture shares a multitude of reasons for why we should give thanks. Whether you're appreciating the friendships in your life, the satisfaction a delicious meal brings, or rejoicing that God's love endures forever, gratitude is an opportunity to remember the Giver. Whatever you may face, God "satisfies the thirsty and fills the hungry with good things" (Psalm 107:9).

C. S. Lewis extolled our endeavors to be more grateful when he said, "We ought to give thanks for all fortune: if it is 'good,' because it is good, if 'bad,' because it works in us patience, humility and the contempt of this world and the hope of our eternal country."[1] Even when you face obstacles, God offers peace and joy that can transcend your circumstances. So take some time each day to embrace the beauty, blessings, and even the trials that you encounter. Perhaps you can find your favorite spot outside in the sunshine to sit with a warm cup of tea, *100 Days of Thanks*, and a pen. Breathe deeply, sip slowly, reflect, and allow your heart and mind to rest a spell and meditate on the fullness of life that surrounds you.

Day 1

Hit Restart

Forgetting what is behind and straining toward what
is ahead, I press on toward the goal to win the prize for
which God has called me heavenward in Christ Jesus.

PHILIPPIANS 3:13–14

Waking up to a beautiful sunrise is so promising. The air is quiet. Birds are beginning to stir in their nests. The moon is fading away as the sun's rays quietly take over the sky. It's as if God hit the restart button and we are powering up for a new day, a new beginning. Our batteries are charged, the things of yesterday are gone, and God is unveiling a chance to start anew. Today is a blank page in a journal—crisp, clean, and ready for a beautiful story to unfold.

Every day, we have the chance to be more patient, more forgiving, more kind, more understanding, and more generous. We can right our wrongs, learn from yesterday's mistakes, listen more, argue less, put down our phones, look at our family, and start over. We will still make mistakes; we won't have everything together or come close to perfection, but God gives us grace, again and again, until we are finally made new.

Hope is not lost. Mercies are abundant. Another day has come.

Mercy is new every morning. Thank God for a
fresh start today.

....

....

....

....

....

Day 2

Creation Bursts
with Beauty

When I consider Your heavens, the work of Your fingers,
the moon and the stars, which You have ordained; . . . O
Lord, our Lord, how majestic is Your name in all the earth!

PSALM 8:3, 9 NASB

Delicate crocuses push through frozen ground; autumn leaves cast a golden hue; foam-tipped waves flash in the sunlight. Does God's creation leave you breathless? Even on the coldest and darkest days, stars shimmer. Giant redwoods stand majestic. God could have created this world to merely be workable, practical. He could have stopped with one type of tree and flower. But He chose to encompass the universe with vast beauty to delight us daily. Praise our loving and gracious Creator!

Today, what do you see in creation that's bursting with beauty?

....

....

....

....

God's Character

"The LORD, the LORD God, compassionate and gracious, slow to anger, and abounding in lovingkindness and truth."
EXODUS 34:6 NASB

God's gifts reflect His character. He is full of grace, compassionate, faithful, all-powerful, merciful, and wise. He is patient, kind, and gentle. Did you see a sick friend begin to heal? God is all-powerful. Did you feel His deep and abiding presence during a low point this week? God is compassionate. Maybe you experienced His forgiveness after deliberately choosing not to obey His Word. God is merciful. Praise the Lord for His perfect character.

What aspects of God's character have you seen and experienced over the past few days?

....

....

Day 4

Cultivating a Habit
of Gratitude

*It is good to praise the Lord . . . , proclaiming your love
in the morning and your faithfulness at night.*

Psalm 92:1—2

We develop some habits at such a young age that we barely notice them today. Brushing teeth, combing hair, and washing hands are taught repeatedly to children until they're well-established habits. Throughout life, we develop more habits, both good and bad. Daily exercise, emotional eating, addiction, saving money, spending money recklessly, saying *please* and *thank you*, avoiding conflict—these habits are all formed over time.

We form cognitive habits, too, like gratitude. Imagine the difference this could make in your daily life. If instead of being frustrated that a meeting ran late, you were thankful for the innovative ideas that were shared. If you soaked in the tenderness of comforting a crying baby at 2:00 a.m. without despairing over lost sleep. Gratitude can change your outlook—and actions—in life-changing ways. It takes practice and some failures; habits don't develop overnight. But by choosing gratitude moment by moment, you'll see it become second nature.

What good habits are you grateful for, and what good things do they bear in your life? What other good habit could you begin cultivating this week?

....

....

....

....

Day 5

7.6 Billion

After this I looked, and there before me was a great
multitude that no one could count, from every nation,
tribe, people and language, standing before the throne
and before the Lamb. They were wearing white robes
and were holding palm branches in their hands. And
they cried out in a loud voice: "Salvation belongs to
our God, who sits on the throne, and to the Lamb."

REVELATION 7:9–10

Our world holds 7.6 billion people,[1] each with different fingerprints, ear shapes, irises, voices, and gaits. Our stories, talents, personalities, creativity, humor, leadership skills, and idiosyncrasies make each of us unique. The world would be monotonous with 7.6 billion clones, wouldn't it? Thankfully God loves diversity. He created a world of different races, languages, customs, and cultures; the differences are beautiful, and they challenge and pull us out of our comfort zones. Thank God for the diverse creation He created.

Name a few things that make you unique.

....

....

....

Thankfully,
God loves
diversity.

The Wonder of the Human Body

Oh yes, you shaped me first inside, then out; you formed
me in my mother's womb. . . . You know me inside
and out, you know every bone in my body; you know
exactly how I was made, bit by bit, how I was sculpted
from nothing into something. Like an open book, you
watched me grow from conception to birth; all the
stages of my life were spread out before you, the days
of my life all prepared before I'd even lived one day.

PSALM 139:13–16 MSG

Let's talk science. How many atoms are in every adult? Around seven octillion. Your body creates seven miles of new blood vessels for every new pound of fat or muscle. The femur is stronger than steel. One step uses up to two hundred muscles. An adult's small intestine measures eight to twenty-three feet. We are unaware of what our body and its systems accomplish second by second to sustain our lives. It's miraculous really.

While this happens, we go about our incredibly busy schedules and expect our bodies to keep up. Until we get a bad diagnosis or a broken bone or our whole family wakes up with strep throat, we don't think about—or are unaware of—the miraculous gift of our bodies.

Now, as you feel your heart beating, remember it beats around one hundred thousand times a day. When you eat, be grateful for your ten thousand taste buds—in two weeks, you'll have a new set. And as your head hits the pillow tonight, stretch your limbs with gratitude, sink under your covers, and say a prayer of thanks and awe for your body and its daily miracles.

We tend to critique our bodies more often than we give thanks for them. Today, think of something about your physical self that you are incredibly grateful for.

....

....

....

....

Day 7

Thanksgiving, Even Without Turkey

"Giving thanks is a sacrifice that truly honors me."
PSALM 50:23 NLT

Television commercials, social media, churches, stores, and more remind us of gratitude as Thanksgiving approaches. And while slicing the turkey and passing the gravy boat, we ritualistically list what we're grateful for. After all, it's Thanksgiving. Ponder this question: Could you carry that mind-set of gratitude through the year, not just in November? Celebrate a daily Thanksgiving with eyes wide-open for God's gifts and a heart full of thanks for every precious blessing in your life.

Pretend you're sitting at the dining room table laden with a full Thanksgiving spread, and Jesus is your dinner company. What would you tell Him?

....

....

....

....

Day 8

Every Relationship Has Significance

I thank my God every time I remember you.

PHILIPPIANS 1:3

Do you have a memory of a stranger, acquaintance, or someone else you didn't know well having a positive impact on your life? Do you remember your kindergarten teacher instructing you on how to read? Or a soccer coach who believed in you—even when you didn't? What about a pastor, therapist, neighbor, or camp counselor? Every relationship, whether for a season or a lifetime, is a unique facet of your life's story. Think about how one of these people, even though he or she may have only briefly crossed paths with you, blessed your life in some way.

Name a few relationships that lasted for only a season but impacted you in great ways.

....

....

Day 9

God Uses All
Things for Good

*You intended to harm me, but God intended
it for good to accomplish what is now being
done, the saving of many lives.*

GENESIS 50:20

It's easy—effortless, even—to have a grateful heart during the happy times, when you're overcome with God's goodness. When you're offered your dream job, repair a broken relationship, or see a loved one healed, rejoicing comes easily. Bad news brings a different reaction. You feel discouraged, fearful, angry, sad, and a threshold of other challenging emotions. You might feel, as the psalmist says in Psalm 119:28, your "soul is weary with sorrow." How can you be grateful in trying times? Is it even possible?

We don't have easy answers; we may not understand until we are with the Lord. But we know and cling to this truth: our pain will not be wasted. Romans 8:28 reminds us, "God causes all things to work together for good" (NASB). Not just some things, but *all things*—the good and the bad. You can be comforted, you can even give thanks and rejoice, because the pain *will* cease. God has already written the end of the story. And it all works together for good.

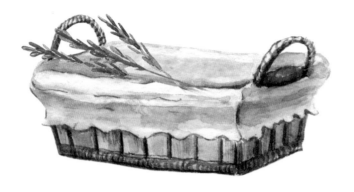

When have you seen God use suffering for good?
Reflect on Romans 8:28.

....

....

....

....

....

....

....

The Light to Our Path

Your word is a lamp for my feet, a light on my path.
PSALM 119:105

It's remarkable the Bible still has relevancy in our modern age of electric cars and video chatting. Though times have changed, the Lord's Word continues to be a light to our every footstep. Its promises bring comfort and hope, it equips us to serve, and its truth renews our minds. It is an invaluable and irreplaceable gift.

What is your favorite Bible verse? How does it shine a light to your path?

....

....

....

....

Mind, Body, and Soul

*May God himself, the God of peace, sanctify you through
and through. May your whole spirit, soul and body be
kept blameless at the coming of our Lord Jesus Christ.*

1 THESSALONIANS 5:23

Mind, *body,* and *soul.* Nothing affects these areas more than gratitude. When we focus our thoughts on God's gifts, we dig a well of deep joy, peace, and contentment. By exercising and eating well, we show care and gratitude for our physical bodies, and studies indicate that thankfulness is beneficial for our health. When we thank our Provider, we nourish and strengthen our spiritual relationship by constantly communing with Him. Gratitude sustains us, mind, body, and soul.

Have you cared for your mind, body, and soul? Or do you neglect any of these areas?

....

....

....

Day 12

It's the Journey, Not the Destination

Keep your eyes open, hold tight to your convictions, give it all you've got, be resolute, and love without stopping.

1 Corinthians 16:13–14 MSG

You've probably heard the phrase, "It's the journey, not the destination." That sentiment is directly applicable to the theme of gratitude. Picture two runners on identical courses. Their goal is the finish line, but their time isn't important; they're running for the enjoyment of the sport. One runner dashes off, her eyes focused on the next mile, then the next, and the next. She is efficient, oblivious to everything but the end. As she sprints forward, her surroundings blur. The other runner knows the course is short and wants to experience it all. She looks around, noticing the brilliant blue sky. She sees familiar faces cheering her on and feels the gentle breeze, soaking it all in. She is present and grateful.

If we go through the day without feeling thankful for anything, it's because we're too focused on the finish line. We aren't looking at the gifts around us. We aren't being present. Life is short. Look up, make eye contact, experience the gifts all around you, and enjoy the run. Remember: it's the journey, not the destination.

Which runner do you relate to the most? How so?

....

....

....

Life, an Undeserved Gift

If you then, who are evil, know how to give good gifts
to your children, how much more will your Father who
is in heaven give good things to those who ask him!

<small>MATTHEW 7:11 ESV</small>

Y ou never anticipate the middle-of-the-night phone call—the one everyone dreads, when you discover your loved one had a heart attack, or a friend was in a car accident, or the cancer took her life. Our lives can change in the blink of an eye. One minute you're eating dinner, mentally going through your to-do list, and the next you're racing to the hospital with your heart pounding and prayers on your lips, knowing life will never be the same. Until we encounter loss or tragedy, we forget how precious life is. We take it for granted, grumble about it, or wish it were different. Friend, all of life is an undeserved gift from the living God. If this week has been stressful, or this year has had more trials than victories, take heart; remember how quickly life can change. Right now, in this very moment, you have the gift of life.

If you knew your life was about to dramatically change, what three things would you say you are presently grateful for?

All of life is an undeserved gift from the living God.

Day 14

When Jesus Gave Thanks

To everyone who is thirsty, he gives something to drink;
to everyone who is hungry, he gives good things to eat.

PSALM 107:9 CEV

Roughly half of Jesus' public prayers in the four Gospels are prayers of thanksgiving for food. He thanked God for five loaves and two fish while feeding the five thousand. When He broke bread for the Last Supper, and when He appeared to the disciples and they fed Him, He thanked the Father. Any time He touched food in the Bible, He gave thanks. Follow the example of Jesus; recognize the Lord is our Great Provider.

How has the Lord provided for you today?

....

....

....

Day 15

He Fills Our Mouths with Laughter

He will yet fill your mouth with laughter,
and your lips with shouting.
JOB 8:21 ESV

When someone said, "Laughter is the best medicine," that writer was onto something. Think about the last time you laughed. How did it make you feel? It's almost impossible to not feel happy and less anxious after laughing. The very act of laughter releases endorphins, lowers stress levels, and quite literally soothes tension in our bodies. Laughter is a gift from God. Job says God fills our mouths with laughter. Praise our good God for the gift of laughter!

When is the last time you were filled with laughter?

....

....

....

....

....

You Don't Need to Have It All Together

"'Love the Lord your God with all your heart, all your soul, all your mind, and all your strength.' The second command is this: 'Love your neighbor as you love yourself.' There are no commands more important than these."

MARK 12:30—31 NCV

There's lots of pressure to "have it all together." We don't want to look like fumbling, messy, disorganized, barely-hanging-on individuals. We want to appear cool, calm, and collected. We want to be supermom and superdad, excel at our jobs, juggle a million balls, have a model home, be respected by others, and look the part.

What if someone told you, "You don't need to have it all together"?

Those words bring relief and freedom, and they offer respite in an outward-focused culture. They are a gift in our demanding world. Scripture tells us the two most important commands in a believer's life are to love God and love others. Hallelujah! Can you do that today? Simply love the Lord and be good to those around you. God lifts any other expectations from the table. You *don't* need to have it all together, dear friend. Take a moment to comprehend this truth. Let your heart sing with gratitude as you extract yourself from what the world expects and dive into God's grace-filled arms.

How does the phrase "You don't need to have it all together" make you feel? How could it change your life?

....

....

....

....

The Breath of Life

*I bless God every chance I get; my
lungs expand with his praise.*

PSALM 34:1 MSG

*I*nhale, exhale. You breathe up to thirty thousand
times a day, yet you don't need to try at all; breathing is instinctual. Imagine how difficult life would
be if you needed to consciously work for every breath,
tens of thousands of times each day. It sounds overwhelming, doesn't it? The Lord breathed life into
you and continues to sustain your life with every
inhale and every exhale. What a relief!

Breathing is one very vital part of life. What are
other vital ways God sustains you each day?

....

....

....

....

....

Day 18

May They Know We are Christians By Our Gratitude

For it is by grace you have been saved, through faith—and this is not from yourselves, it is the gift of God—not by works, so that no one can boast.
EPHESIANS 2:8–9

If someone asked you to list characteristics of a Christian, what would you say? Words like *patient*, *selfless*, *forgiving*, *humble*, *honest*, *loving*, *joyful*, *generous*, and *compassionate* may come to mind. What about *gratitude*? We have reason to celebrate; God gave up His only Son to give us everything. What an undeserved gift! May unrestrained gratitude mark the life of every believer.

When a friend describes you, would the characteristic of gratitude be mentioned? Do you know someone who embodies a grateful life?

....

....

....

Our God Is in Control

"Do not fear, for I am with you; do not be dismayed,
for I am your God. I will strengthen you and help you;
I will uphold you with my righteous right hand."

ISAIAH 41:10

I'm worried ___ will happen. How often do you think that? We spend time, energy, and emotion on things that may never happen. *What if I don't like my teacher? What if I mess up during this presentation? What if the test results come back positive?*

Worries all have something in common: They're focused on the future. Worry imagines future possible consequences, but many times, we learn our worry was in vain, and we move on to the next worrisome item.

Worry gives us the illusion of control, yet, we only control our choices—nothing else. It's a humbling thought, but there is great freedom in it because *God is in control*. He has always been in control and He will always be in control. Isn't it a relief? Our Father wants us to be without burden. He wants us to be free from worry. With Him in control, we can give up fear. Today, when you find yourself worrying, turn your heart toward God and thank Him for having everything under control.

What are you worrying about or trying to control today?

....

....

....

....

Day 20

The First Ten Minutes
of the Morning

Let the morning bring me word of your unfailing
love, for I have put my trust in you. Show me the
way I should go, for to you I entrust my life.

PSALM 143:8

The first ten minutes of your morning impact the day's tone and your attitude. Consider this scenario: You wake up to your alarm, already frustrated. You stayed up way too late the night before and are paying for it. As you roll out of bed, your mind begins calculating all you need to do. Feeling overwhelmed by everything on your list, you shuffle into the kitchen only to find an empty bag of coffee. Those first ten minutes sound like the prelude to a frustrating, harried, and stressful day.

But what if the first ten minutes were completely different? You wake up to your alarm and feel exhausted, but you smile, thinking of the late night spent with friends. The fatigue is worth it. You get out of bed, breathe deeply, and commit to a positive day. You do your morning ritual of thanking God for the day's blessings, and when you realize there's no coffee, you thank Him for the "necessity" of driving through Starbucks.

The first ten minutes are a launching pad into the day. Invite gratitude on board right away.

Describe the first ten minutes of your day today.
What do you wish they looked like?

....

....

....

....

Day 21

Today Gives Us New Reasons for Praise

With the loving mercy of our God, a new
day from heaven will dawn upon us.
LUKE 1:78 NCV

Until today, you have never experienced this day. It's untouched, unknown. But you can be sure it's packed with new blessings and new reasons to praise our always-generous God. Second Corinthians 5:17 says, "Behold, new things have come" (NASB). The sun rose with many more opportunities for God to bless you—and more reasons to worship Him!

Think about yesterday's events. How did God bless you? What do you hope today holds?

....

....

The Impact of Inventors

*All of Israel stood, and the priests and the Levites played
their instruments to the Eternal One while other priests
standing across from them played trumpets. (King
David had made these instruments and used them
to praise the Eternal, whose love endures forever.)*
2 CHRONICLES 7:6 THE VOICE

The word *inventor* evokes big names, like Thomas Edison, Benjamin Franklin, Bill Gates, or Steve Jobs. There are also inventors whose names are unfamiliar, yet their inventions impact our lives in big and small ways. Without them we wouldn't have dishwashers, pianos, ice cream, and roller coasters. Insulin would be a foreign concept. The Rubik's Cube, windshield wipers, flushing toilets, batteries, and X-rays would not exist. Thank the Lord for all inventors He created and the gifts they invented!

Which inventions are you most grateful for?
Thank God for their presence in your life.

....

....

....

....

All Creatures Great and Small

How many are your works, Lord! In wisdom you made them all; the earth is full of your creatures. There is the sea, vast and spacious, teeming with creatures beyond number—living things both large and small.

Psalm 104:24–25

Have you ever stopped to thank God for bats? Squirrels? Fish? Wildlife benefits us in so many ways. Here are just a few: fish clean oceans, fight climate change, and contribute important nutrients to marine ecosystems. Bats—often feared or disliked—control pests. One brown bat can consume up to a thousand mosquitos an hour. Their pest-eating saves billions of dollars of crops each year and reduces the need for chemical-laden pesticides. Bats also pollinate more than five hundred plant species that provide foods such as mangoes, bananas, cocoa, cashews, vanilla, and figs.

Squirrels steal your birdseed and tear holes in your roof. Annoying. But without them, your backyard may not have that giant oak tree. Squirrels don't always remember where they stored nuts and seeds underground, and their forgotten pantries turn into trees. Trees are dependent on squirrels for scattering their acorns. Did you know an acorn grows best when away from its parent tree?

Our rain forests, savannas, woodlands, seas, deserts, and mountains are teeming with wild animals created by the Lord. Praise God for creatures great and small!

What wildlife mentioned above are you most grateful for now that you know their purpose?

....

....

....

Day 24

God's Marvelous Workmanship

*Each of you should use whatever gift you have
received to serve others, as faithful stewards
of God's grace in its various forms.*

1 PETER 4:10

God created billions of people, each with specific skills and talents. There are athletes, mathematicians, gardeners, salespeople, and teachers. Some are skilled at comforting the grieving, others at captivating audiences, developing software, or handling taxes. If we all were extremely proficient in mathematics, would we have any novels? Or if God only created chefs, who would build a house? Praise our Maker, who created each person with a unique purpose and specific abilities. His "workmanship is marvelous" (Psalm 139:14 NLT).

You have talents; are you using them? If you're not sure what they are, ask the Lord to reveal them to you. What talents do you appreciate in others?

....

....

....

Day 25

Nature Sings

The heavens proclaim the glory of God.
The skies display his craftsmanship.
PSALM 19:1 NLT

Psalm 66 tells us "all the earth worships . . . [and] sings praises" to God (v. 4 CEB). People, trees, birds, deer, stars, streams, and His entire creation can't help but glorify the Creator. Scripture urges, "Come and see God's deeds" because "his works for human beings are awesome" (v. 5 CEB). Let God's awesome deeds fill your heart. Lift your voice with all of nature to join the massive chorus of gratitude to our heavenly Father.

What parts of nature cause you to thank God
for His beautiful work? Why?

....

....

....

The Letter from Paul

Keep your lives free from the love of money and be
content with what you have, because God has said,
"Never will I leave you; never will I forsake you."

<small>HEBREWS 13:5</small>

If the apostle Paul were alive today, he would have been wise to buy Forever stamps when they first emerged, because he was a letter writer. Philippians is one of his most personal letters. It is bursting with joy, gratitude, and encouragement—and he was likely imprisoned while penning the letter.

In Philippians 4 he expressed satisfaction with "whatever the circumstances" (v. 11). Whether he was poor or wealthy, when he had plenty of food or when he was hungry, Paul wrote, "I have learned to be content" (v. 11). Note, this didn't come naturally at first; he had to learn this mind-set of contentment. And he came to realize in every single circumstance, including persecution, hunger, and poverty, he could be content because he had the gift of the Lord's presence—and that was enough.

Paul was full of deep gratitude and joy even in the face of terrible circumstances because he was grateful for the one true Satisfier: the Lord. God was all Paul needed to be content.

Is the gift of Christ enough for you?

....

....

....

....

....

Be the Lone Leper

One of them, when he saw that he was healed, came back
to Jesus, shouting, "Praise God!" He fell to the ground
at Jesus' feet, thanking him for what he had done.
LUKE 17:15–16 NLT

Jesus and His disciples were journeying to Jerusalem. On their way they saw ten lepers standing at a distance—social outcasts with great physical and emotional pain who were required to wear torn clothes and shout, "Unclean! Unclean!" as a warning to others.

Jesus healed the lepers. Imagine the impact this would have on these men; it would be radical, and they would be accepted into society and reunited with family. You probably know the rest of Luke 17. Of the ten healed lepers, only one came back to thank Jesus. Jesus asked, "Didn't I heal ten men? Where are the other nine?" (v. 17 NLT). It seems absurd that the nine didn't return to thank Him after such a life-changing miracle. But when we look at our own lives, it becomes painfully obvious we are ungrateful too. When God gives us a gift, it's very easy to receive it, but life is distracting, and we forget to acknowledge the Giver of all gifts. What would it look like if you were swift to thank the Lord? Look to the one leper as an example, and be someone who always returns to praise God.

Is there a time you were like the nine lepers and forgot to thank the Lord for a gift?

....

....

....

....

....

He Is Ever Present

*As for me, it is good to be near God. I have
made the Sovereign LORD my refuge.*
PSALM 73:28

The Bible promises, "The LORD is close to the brokenhearted and saves those who are crushed in
spirit" (Psalm 34:18). What a comfort, what a gift. We
have all experienced pain or sorrow. Dear believer,
cling to this truth: "The Father of mercies and God
of all comfort" is with you. You are not forgotten. He
"comforts us in all our affliction" (2 Corinthians 1:3,
4 ESV). He is our ever-present God.

When has the Lord seemed especially present to
you?

....

....

....

Day 29

Gratitude Defeats Darkness

Again Jesus spoke to them, saying, "I am the light
of the world. Whoever follows me will never walk
in darkness but will have the light of life."

<small>JOHN 8:12 NRSV</small>

In 2 Chronicles 20, King Jehoshaphat knew a large and powerful army was approaching. God directed him on what to do—and do you know who led His people into battle? The singers and worshippers. They were at the front lines, facing a strong army, and proclaiming, "Give thanks to the LORD, for his steadfast love endures forever" (v. 21 ESV). Gratitude holds tremendous power, and darkness cannot stand against it.

How can you use gratitude to stand against darkness? How can you turn a complaint into praise?

....

....

....

....

What Does Suffering Produce?

In alert expectancy such as this, we're never left feeling shortchanged. Quite the contrary—we can't round up enough containers to hold everything God generously pours into our lives through the Holy Spirit!

ROMANS 5:5 MSG

R eal gratitude doesn't allow picking and choosing what we're thankful for. Instead, we're told to give thanks in all circumstances (1 Thessalonians 5:18). Note, *all circumstances* encompass everything—not just the good stuff! Gratitude is easy when you're told the cancer is gone, but what if it comes back? If your child makes the soccer team, you celebrate, but what if he's cut? Marrying someone you love is a gift, but is heartbreak? Friend, it is hard to give thanks in all circumstances. Some days it may feel totally impossible. It takes time to get to the point of gratitude.

But hear these words: In Romans 5 Paul rejoices in suffering. *What? Why?!* Paul knew suffering ultimately produced good. "We know how troubles can develop passionate patience in us, and how that patience in turn forges the tempered steel of virtue, keeping us alert for whatever God will do next" (vv.3–4 MSG). Other Scripture versions say suffering brings endurance, perseverance, character, and hope—and in those we can rejoice!

Do you pick and choose what you're grateful for?

....

....

....

....

One Egg or a Dozen

"What father among you, if his son asks for a fish, will instead of a fish give him a serpent; or if he asks for an egg, will give him a scorpion? If you then, who are evil, know how to give good gifts to your children, how much more will the heavenly Father give the Holy Spirit to those who ask him!"

Luke 11:11–13 ESV

Do you know the story in Luke involving a father, a son, and gifts of eggs and fish? In it Jesus gave a great visual of God's love for us and the gifts He provides. If someone we love deeply (children, parents, best friend, spouse, grandparents) asks for an egg, we would give that loved one an egg—or even a dozen, if we're able. We certainly wouldn't think to hand someone we claim to love a stinging, eight-legged, poisonous scorpion. What kind of gift is that? It's dangerous. Likewise, if someone asks for bread, we wouldn't hand over a slithering snake in its place—that would be pointless.

God loves us so much more than we can comprehend, and when He gives us gifts, He always gives what is best for us. We can trust He hears and answers our requests, and He will not respond with useless or harmful gifts, like a scorpion or snake. If we, as humans, can give good gifts to those we love, how much more can God, the Creator of the universe and rescuer of our souls?

What is the best material gift you've received, and given? Why?

....

....

....

....

....

....

....

....

Day 32

This Is How to Thank the Lord

Shout with joy to the LORD, all the earth! Worship
the LORD with gladness. Come before him, singing with joy.
Acknowledge that the LORD is God! He made us, and we
are his. We are his people, the sheep of his pasture. Enter
his gates with thanksgiving; go into his courts with
praise. Give thanks to him and praise his name. For
the LORD is good. His unfailing love continues forever,
and his faithfulness continues to each generation.
PSALM 100 NLT

The book of Psalms is bursting with praise and ado-
ration for God, but only one psalm is singled out
as a psalm of thanksgiving. Psalm 100 is a beautiful
example of *how* to thank our Lord. We are to *shout* with
joy, *worship* Him with gladness, *sing* for joy, *acknowledge*
His greatness, and *enter* His presence with thanksgiving. Why? Because He is good, His love never fails, and
He is faithful.

The next few mornings, read Psalm 100 to begin
your day. How will you show God gratitude today?

....

....

The Gift of Relationships

Let us consider how we may spur one another on toward love and good deeds, not giving up meeting together, as some are in the habit of doing, but encouraging one another—and all the more as you see the Day approaching.

HEBREWS 10:24–25

If you were the only person on earth, you would be quite lonely, right? You wouldn't have anyone to cry or laugh with, talk to, or learn from; it would just be you. Solitary. Solo. A lifetime completely alone is almost unimaginable. Our relationships with others are a central part of life, and they shape us in countless ways. Thank God for the gift of relationships, and praise Him, the Most High King, for being in relationship with you.

How can you strengthen your relationships with others?

....

....

....

One Powerful Word

*Be filled with the Spirit . . . always giving thanks to God the
Father for everything, in the name of our Lord Jesus Christ.*
EPHESIANS 5:18, 20

Consider the difference between the following: I *have*
to go for a run versus I *get* to go for a run. By changing one word, the connotation switches from negative
to positive. You don't *have* to; you *get* to. There are things
we typically need to do: pay bills, mow the lawn, work
late some nights, do the dishes. But instead of framing
everything with a *have*-to mind-set, what if you adopt a
get-to outlook? If you *get to* pay the bills, you have money
in the bank; if you *get* to mow the lawn, you are healthy
enough to exert yourself. You *get* to work overtime, and
it's not always fun, but it might mean you are earning
a bigger paycheck. You *get* to do the dishes because you
have food in your home. See the drastic difference a
simple word can make?

Take control over your words and try replacing *I
have to* with *I get to* this week. Watch how the tasks you
dread will begin feeling less like obligations and more
like gifts.

What are a few things you have to do? Replace
them with I get to and see how your perspective
changes.

Spotting the Small Things

You shower him with blessings that last forever; he finds joy in knowing Your presence and loving You.

PSALM 21:6 THE VOICE

Family, food, a home, a job: these blessings are at the top of every gratitude list. But what about smaller, subtler gifts you may overlook? Your children's laughter, unexpected snail mail, the burst of pomegranate seeds in your mouth. The sunlight illuminating morning dew. The comfort of your couch, Amazon Prime, the steaming warmth of your coffee mug. Your favorite shampoo. These are small gifts with an everyday impact. Praise God for the small things.

Look around; what five small gifts can you spot?

....

....

....

Day 36

There Is No One Like You, Lord

There is none like you, O LORD, and
there is no God besides you.
1 CHRONICLES 17:20 ESV

Who is like our God? Our Lord is wise, sovereign, holy, loving, and faithful. He is merciful and gracious, just, omniscient, and all-powerful. He is infinite. He is perfect. He is the King of kings. There is no one like Him. Let's praise Him with the words of Hannah: "There is no one holy like the LORD. There is no God but you; there is no Rock like our God" (1 Samuel 2:2 NCV).

Which of God's attributes are you most grateful for today?

....

....

....

....

....

Where's the Next Gift?

*And my God will supply all your needs according
to His riches in glory in Christ Jesus.*
PHILIPPIANS 4:19 NASB

Think of a five-year-old waiting to open presents at his birthday party. He excitedly tears open the wrapping paper on the first gift and tosses it aside for the next. Anyone knows that when you receive a gift, a *thank-you* is courteous, and often, expected. But sometimes, like the five-year-old, we simply receive a gift, and then look around for the next. We forget the gifts we have, and we want more to unwrap. Think about your day or week so far. What can you give thanks for? Maybe you successfully completed a work project or smoothed things over with a coworker. Did you receive an extralong hug from your child, hear good news at the doctor, or enjoy a meal at your favorite restaurant? Perhaps you simply survived a long, tough week that seemed neverending. Instead of looking ahead to tomorrow, which holds more gifts, stop and acknowledge the blessings already in front of you. Savor them. And say *thank you*.

In the past few days, when did you feel joy or relief? Reflect on those moments and give thanks.

....

....

The Greatest Gift

I shall give thanks to You, for You have answered
me, and You have become my salvation.

PSALM 118:21 NASB

The greatest gift we will ever receive is salvation. Jesus, our Great Rescuer, died so we could live. He selflessly lived on earth and suffered greatly for our deliverance. Have you stopped to ponder the mercy of salvation? Gratitude for salvation is all over the Bible's pages. Psalm 118 focuses on this gift, and its title is "Thanksgiving for the LORD's Saving Goodness" (NASB). Psalm 18:46 states, "The LORD lives! Praise to my Rock! May the God of my salvation be exalted!" (NLT). The psalmist in Psalm 96:2 encourages daily thanksgiving: "Sing to the LORD; praise his name. Each day proclaim the good news that he saves" (NLT). The precious gift of salvation changes us forever. In fact, Revelation 7 says we will still be praising Jesus for this gift in heaven. It describes people "from every nation and all tribes and peoples and tongues" (v. 9 NASB) standing before the Lord. "They cry out with a loud voice, saying 'Salvation to our God who sits on the throne, and to the Lamb'" (v. 10 NASB). It truly is the greatest gift.

If someone asked how the gift of salvation has changed your life, what would you say?

Day 39

Something Extraordinary Is Always Happening

God does wonders that cannot be understood; he does so many miracles they cannot be counted.

JOB 5:9 NCV

You might think you live a relatively ordinary life. But the truth is, no one does. Moment by moment, we are experiencing the extraordinary. Our eye has more than two million parts, and when you look at gray clouds in the sky, it is distinguishing between five hundred shades of gray. Your peace lily plant is cleaning the air, and the banana you ate for breakfast is working to lower your blood pressure. Every moment, something extraordinary is happening.

Praise God for the extraordinary ways He's working in your life right now.

....

....

....

Gratitude Spurs Us On

*For they refreshed my spirit and yours
also. Such men deserve recognition.*

1 CORINTHIANS 16:18

They never thank me for anything around here. Does that thought sound familiar? You worked overtime while your boss was on vacation. You did five loads of laundry for your teenagers. You stayed up all night helping a friend study. We don't serve others to be thanked, but gratitude helps spur us on, and it makes "yes" easier next time. Gratitude says, "I see you. I value you. Thank you."

Who do you need to spur on this week? How?

....

....

....

Day 41

On Coffee and Gatorade: We Pursue What Won't Satisfy

"Do not store up for yourselves treasures on earth,
where moth and rust destroy, and where thieves break
in and steal. But store up for yourselves treasures
in heaven, where neither moth nor rust destroys,
and where thieves do not break in or steal; for where
your treasure is, there your heart will be also."

MATTHEW 6:19–21 NASB

Cravings are powerful. If a pregnant woman wants pineapple, a brown and speckled banana won't satiate her, and she probably won't say thank you. But when you give her pineapple, she'll be gratefully ecstatic. Say you run a half marathon in ninety-degree weather, and at the finish line you're handed a medal and . . . a steaming cup of coffee. A hot beverage isn't going to satisfy your desire for something cold, and you certainly won't be grateful for it. But if you receive a thermos full of Gatorade, you're immediately appreciative.

Although these examples seem silly, they ring true in our journey to gratitude. We try to quench our deep longings with material things that will never give us contentment. We try to eat bananas when our bodies crave pineapple. We drink coffee instead of Gatorade.

Pursue Jesus.
He will satisfy.

So, instead of being satisfied, we crave even more. And more. And more. Without pursuing our truest craving—Jesus Christ—we cannot know and experience real and fulfilling gratitude. Pursue Jesus. He will satisfy.

Who or what do you turn to in an effort to fill your deep longings?

....

....

....

....

Day 42

Weather: More than Small Talk

"Then I will give you rain in due season, and the land shall yield her increase, and the trees of the field shall yield their fruit."

LEVITICUS 26:4 KJV

ook outside. Is it sunny and hot, gray and drizzly, cloudy, breezy, or snowy? Give thanks, for each kind of weather has its benefits. The sun warms our skin and increases vitamin D in our bodies, cloudy days help us think more clearly, snow insulates the soil, and rain nurtures the food we eat. Freezing temperatures kill disease-carrying bugs, and wind helps generate clean energy. Weather is more than small talk. Praise God for His goodness and wisdom in creating different types of weather.

What is today's weather like? What are five ways it's beautiful or beneficial?

....

....

....

....

A Small Thank-You Makes a Big Impact

May you be richly rewarded by the LORD, the God of Israel.
RUTH 2:12

You are surrounded by people to thank: the barista making your morning latte and the cab driver who gets you to the airport on time. Your always-prompt mail carrier, the professor who patiently answers your questions, and the kind customer service representative at Target. Thank the bus driver who safely transports your children to school, or the waiter who accommodates your late party. A simple thank-you and a smile, a conversation, a generous tip—these acknowledgments make a big and bright impact.

Keep your eyes open for those you can thank. Does anyone come to mind now?

....

....

....

....

Day 44

God-Given Emotions

The LORD has appeared of old to me, saying: "Yes, I
have loved you with an everlasting love; therefore
with lovingkindness I have drawn you."

JEREMIAH 31:3 NKJV

Life would look very different without emotions. What if we didn't know joy, delight, excitement, and satisfaction? What if we couldn't express ourselves or feel anything in situations in which we would normally feel angry, sad, or mournful?

Emotions are God-given. The Bible speaks of God's anger, compassion, and love. He doesn't ignore our emotions; He responds to them. Psalm 34 says, "The LORD is close to the brokenhearted and saves those who are crushed in spirit" (v. 18). He is gracious and compassionate and rejoices over His beloved.

While on earth Jesus displayed emotion. He wept at the tomb of His friend Lazarus. He was surprised, amazed, angry, and distressed. He was moved with compassion by many: two blind men, a widow by her son's coffin, a hungry crowd, a leper. As you can see, Jesus didn't always feel happy, and He didn't suppress His emotions. The Lord doesn't expect us to only feel joy. We can be honest about our emotions, whether we are feeling excited and hopeful or full of grief. Praise God for our emotions and the freedom we have to express them!

Do you feel pressure to constantly be joyful? Do you ever stuff your emotions down? Remember they are a gift from God—an instrument to express ourselves.

....

....

....

The Blessings of Grass Stains

Give thanks to the LORD, for he is good;
his love endures forever.
PSALM 107:1

Pour in detergent, select the settings, load the clothes, turn on the washer, switch to the dryer, fold, stack, and repeat. Procter & Gamble says the average American family does 300–390 loads of laundry per year, and while you may do much more or less, the point is: laundry never ends. As long as you have clothing, you'll have items to wash. Since laundry is a steady soundtrack in our lives, how can we turn it into a song of gratitude instead of drudgery?

When treating the grass stains on your son's jeans, thank God for your strong and healthy boy. If your spouse's work uniform makes a constant appearance, it signifies a job and a steady paycheck. Sheets and pillowcases represent a bed to sleep on, and bath towels mean you have the luxury of a shower in your home. Even life's most mundane chores reflect God's many blessings in our lives. During your next load of laundry, look at the pile and remember: it's a godsend.

What's your least favorite household chore? How can you change your perspective regarding that task?

....

....

....

Day 46

Ordinary Is a Blessing

Every good and perfect gift is from above, coming down from the Father of the heavenly lights.

JAMES 1:17

We're attracted to the shiny and grandiose. We like big moments and adventurous stories. *Ordinary* sounds boring. Yet, if our child is hospitalized, we yearn for ordinary life. When we're pushed out of our routine by a stressful workweek, tragedy, an emergency, or nonstop busyness, *normal* sounds like perfection, right? Consider this: Mary and Joseph were ordinary people, and Jesus entered our world in an ordinary way—through childbirth. Ordinary is holy. Ordinary is grace. Ordinary is a gift.

In what ways are you thankful for your ordinary life?

....

....

....

....

....

Day 47

A Gift or a Disappointment?

Whatever you do, whether in word or deed,
do it all in the name of the Lord Jesus, giving
thanks to God the Father through him.

COLOSSIANS 3:17

I s the glass half-empty or half-full? Daily you choose one or the other by living with gratitude or ingratitude. You decide to see the water as a gift or as a disappointment and choose to give thanks for what you have—or focus on what you lack. *You* make the choice. Let's fill our half-full cups and keep filling them with focus on what our heavenly Father gives us.

Write down some half-empty thoughts. How can you make them half-full instead?

....

....

....

....

....

It's More than a Dirty Dish

I will offer to you the sacrifice of thanksgiving
and call on the name of the Lord.
PSALM 116:17 ESV

Lemon-scented dish soap, sunshine streaming through the window. You smile and relish washing the dishes, crusted with last night's spaghetti. You just love having piles and piles of dishes to wash. Hmmm. Is that how you feel when you do the dishes? Most of us would likely reply with a hearty "No!" We'd rather be relaxing in a bubble bath, not bathing the dishes, right?

Yet, if you look for it, there is joy even in cleaning our dishes. As you pick up another dish, recall the lively conversation that happened over the spaghetti dinner. Give thanks for the hot water you're using to clean the dishes. While you scrub the silverware, recall the friends who have sat around your table, breaking bread together and laughing until you cry. Let gratitude envelop your whole being as you try to scour that one pesky dish, for you had food on your table last night and your loved ones went to bed with full bellies and nourished bodies. Every dirty dish is more than simply a dirty dish; it's a representation of God's blessings.

Think of the last time you washed dishes. What blessings were hiding in the stacks of plates and glasses?

....

....

....

....

....

Day 49

Accept the Gift
of Relaxation

*"Come to me, all of you who are tired and have
heavy loads, and I will give you rest."*
MATTHEW 11:28 NCV

What if you ended a long, harried, exhausting week, and you were told, "Congratulations! You made it! Now, to relax, you can throw a birthday party with fourteen kindergartners on a sugar high, or you can run errands in the ninety-five-degree heat." Sounds like the opposite of relaxation, doesn't it?

Instead, how would you choose to relax? What helps your shoulders loosen up and your jaw unclench? How do you take a figurative deep breath?

Yoga, a long run, walking with a friend, or being by yourself are some examples. For others, it's being outdoors in nature or on the couch with a pair of knitting needles. It could be reading, taking a long bath, lighting lavender candles, or eating dark chocolate while watching a movie. Maybe it's laughing with family or sharing dinner with close friends.

What would life be like without these gifts? God gives us these different ways to relax for our enjoyment and well-being. If you're resisting the gift of relaxation, now is the time to embrace it!

What's your favorite way to relax? How do you experience the Lord through it?

....

....

....

Day 50

Don't Forget!

Bless the LORD, O my soul, and forget none of His benefits; who pardons all your iniquities, who heals all your diseases; who redeems your life from the pit, who crowns you with lovingkindness and compassion; who satisfies your years with good things, so that your youth is renewed like the eagle.

PSALM 103:2–5 NASB

I n Psalm 103 David wrote down reminders of the Lord's works as if he were thinking, *Don't forget! Remember all of this!* David implored his soul to recall God's forgiveness, healing, redemption, love, kindness, and compassion. He wrote with detail to retain every facet of the Lord's faithfulness. Like David we are forgetful! We need to write down and remind ourselves of God's providence in our lives.

What is one way you've seen God's provision this year? Write about it in detail.

....

....

....

....

The Easy Road and the Hard Road

There is a way that seems right to a man,
but its end is the way to death.
PROVERBS 14:12 ESV

Gratitude is hard. It requires discipline, practice, and perseverance. It's a steep and rocky road, but that in itself is a gift. Its challenges slow you down, enabling you to see the surrounding beauty you may have missed otherwise. Complaining, on the other hand, feels good momentarily. You gain validation, gratification, and you blow off steam. It's an easy road, but it's full of flat concrete with nothing else in sight. It leads nowhere. Which road will you choose today?

Describe how you feel when grateful. Then write down how complaining makes you feel.

....

....

....

Day 52

Make It Doable

So that you may live a life worthy of the Lord and please
him in every way: bearing fruit in every good work, growing
in the knowledge of God, being strengthened with all
power according to his glorious might so that you may
have great endurance and patience, and giving joyful
thanks to the Father, who has qualified you to share in
the inheritance of his holy people in the kingdom of light.

COLOSSIANS 1:10–12

It's time to get in shape. You decide to buy new workout clothes; cut out gluten, dairy, sugar, and all processed foods; join a gym and work out six days a week; buy a treadmill desk to use between 8:00 a.m. and 5:00 p.m.; and ditch driving your car because you're going to ride your bike to work. If you haven't exercised in a while, making too many drastic life changes all at the same time isn't sustainable. But what if you changed one small thing at a time? What if you decided to drink only water for thirty days or walk three days a week? That seems more doable.

The same concept rings true when making gratitude part of your lifestyle. Tiny changes help transform you completely. You can't wake up one morning and decide to never again utter a complaint; you would get frustrated—it's hard work. It takes practice, prayer, and lots of grace for yourself. Try monitoring your complaining for one hour a day or write down five things you are grateful for.

With small changes and consistency, you'll get there, one step at a time.

What is one small change you can make today for a more gratitude-filled life?

....

....

....

The Produce of Our Hearts

Therefore by Him let us continually offer the sacrifice of praise to God, that is, the fruit of our lips, giving thanks to His name.

HEBREWS 13:15 NKJV

A fruit's quality depends on the plant or tree it originates from. A dried-out strawberry plant can't produce sweet and juicy berries, and a diseased apple tree won't bear flavorful apples. In Luke Jesus says, "A person full of goodness in his heart produces good things" (6:45 THE VOICE). What fruit does your heart bear? Are you quick to be grateful, encouraging, and content, or are your words scarred with complaints and bruised with discontentment? Examine the produce of your heart today, and cultivate it to bear good fruit.

What fruit have you been bearing lately?

....

....

What's All This Noise?

Now stand here and see the great
thing the LORD is about to do.
1 SAMUEL 12:16 NLT

Lots of voices clamor for our attention: worry, stress, frustration, distraction, exhaustion, perfection, and more. They're noisy. They tend to drown out gratitude, and it's hard to silence them. Once they begin chattering, good luck—they like to talk. They will only stop when edged out by other voices: thankfulness, perspective, hope, joy, peace, and contentment. It's harder to get those voices to speak up, but once they do, you'll want to hear them forever. Stand still and listen—who is making more noise?

What voices speak loudest in your life? What do you want to hear instead?

....

....

....

....

....

When Heaven-Sent Bread Is Not Enough

Now, Israel, this is what the LORD your God
wants you to do: Respect the LORD your God, and
do what he has told you to do. Love him. Serve
the LORD your God with your whole being.

DEUTERONOMY 10:12 NCV

In a series of miraculous events, God graciously delivered the Israelites from slavery under the Egyptians. Freedom! While traveling in the wilderness, the Israelites were hungry, so God did something amazing: every day, He sent bread from heaven, called manna. Bread raining from the sky! But eventually, manna was not enough. The people complained, "Oh, how we wish that the Lord had just put us to death while we were still in the land of Egypt. There we could sit by the pots cooking meat and eat our fill of bread" (Exodus 16:3 CEB). The Israelites missed the food they ate in Egypt *when they were slaves.*

Instead of thanking God for freedom, safety, and provision, the Israelites complained and whined. When they should have been marveling at the Lord's goodness, the Israelites revealed their ungrateful hearts. What about you? In our culture today, we want *more* and *better* and we never have enough—just like the Israelites. Are

you continually asking God for more, more, and more?
Or are you mindful of the manna God has given you?

How often do you ask God for "more," and how
often do you praise Him for the manna you
already have?

....

....

....

....

....

....

Day 56

Work Is a Gift, Not a Curse

May your deeds be shown to your servants, your splendor to their children. May the favor of the Lord our God rest on us; establish the work of our hands for us.

PSALM 90:16–17

What would it be like to never work? Your activities could include napping, watching Netflix, playing on your phone, and lazing around; you would never cook dinner, clock in to a job, or sit in a strategy meeting. That sounds great . . . for a few days, but probably not for a lifetime. God created us to work, produce, and have purpose, and He began with Adam.

Genesis 2 says the garden of Eden had "trees that were pleasing to the eye and good for food" (v. 9). God told Adam to "work it and take care of it" (v. 15). Later He tasked Adam with naming all the animals.

You'll notice all sorts of occupations in the Bible. David was a shepherd (and Saul's harp player), Jesus was a carpenter, Peter fished, Lydia sold purple dye, and Matthew collected taxes. Notice these Bible characters were all significant, but their jobs were "normal" jobs. Other people were tentmakers, farmers, bakers, and soldiers. Whether you stay at home with your kids, volunteer, run a company, teach, assist a VP, or pastor a church, every job is a gift.

Do you think of your job as a gift? What holds
you back from thinking of it in this way?

....

....

....

Day 57

The Beloved Gift of Friends

"I no longer call you servants, because a servant does not know his master's business. Instead, I have called you friends, for everything that I learned from my Father I have made known to you."

JOHN 15:15

The Bible describes some very special friendships. Risking his own life, Jonathan protected David from Saul. Ruth and Naomi mourned together, and loyalty marked their relationship. Jesus forgave Peter time after time. Mary and Elizabeth shared joy over miraculous pregnancies. Elisha wouldn't let Elijah travel alone. These friendships were based on respect, love, trust, loyalty, understanding, shared experiences, and grace. Friends are beloved gifts and irreplaceable companions—gifts from our Lord, who calls us friends.

Who are a couple of your special friendships? How did the Lord bring them into your life?

....

....

....

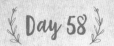

Come Away and Rest

*He said to them, "Come with me by yourselves
to a quiet place and get some rest."*
MARK 6:31

In Genesis God demonstrates the importance of rest by taking a break—a sabbath—from creating. He shows us work and rest are good and necessary. When you cram too much into your week and don't stop for a sabbath, you soon feel frazzled, overwhelmed, and exhausted. Our bodies, minds, and souls need rest, and our Father offers us the beautiful, rejuvenating gift of the Sabbath.

Do you take a sabbath? How can you keep that time sacred and actually rest?

....

....

....

....

....

....

The Veil Has Been Torn

*So, brothers and sisters, we are completely free to
enter the Most Holy Place without fear because of
the blood of Jesus' death. We can enter through a
new and living way that Jesus opened for us.*

HEBREWS 10:19–20 NCV

We can go before the Lord in prayer at any time. We can talk to Him in our car, while cleaning, doing laundry, or mowing the lawn. We can whisper prayers during a sleepless night, cry out loudly in joy or pain. We can approach Him with boldness. Our access to Him is instantaneous.

While this type of communing with the Lord sounds like everyday prayer to us, it was vastly different before Jesus gave His life. Only the high priest could enter the Holy of Holies (God's presence), and it happened only once a year. Beforehand the high priest had to perform a ritual that included cleansing, specific clothing, incense, sacrificial animals, and more. But when Jesus shed His blood for our sins and the veil separating the Holy of Holies from the Holy Place was torn, everyone gained access to the Lord.

Imagine engaging in a routine that involved special clothing and animal sacrifices before you could talk to God. What a difference Jesus' blood makes! Praise God that we, as sinners, have unlimited access to Him at any moment.

Have you ever realized your ability to communicate with God is a gift? When do you most often talk to Him?

....

....

....

He Will Not Slumber

He will not let your foot be moved; he who keeps
you will not slumber. Behold, he who keeps Israel
will neither slumber nor sleep. The LORD is your
keeper; the LORD is your shade on your right hand.

PSALM 121:3–5 ESV

It's impossible to be actively present in someone else's life 24/7. We go to work, run errands, have doctor's appointments, and attend social functions. Plus, we all need sleep. There's only One who is always present. Our faithful Father watches over us while we're sleeping. He never slumbers. He's never distracted. God's constant and never-ending presence is one of the most comforting gifts we can ever possess!

Reflect on the past week. In which situations were you glad for God's never-ending presence?

....

....

....

....

....

Day 61

Your Favorite Place
in the House

*Now My eyes will be open and My ears attentive to
prayer made in this place. For now have I chosen and
sanctified this house, that My name may be there forever;
and My eyes and My heart will be there perpetually.*
2 Chronicles 7:15–16 nkjv

Some say the kitchen is their spot. They experience a tangible release of tension while stirring and slicing. Others love their quiet bedroom. They can shut the door and have uninterrupted time alone. Some favor the front porch, breathing the morning air as the earth rouses. What is your favorite place in the house? Praise God for the blessing of a roof over your head and a place of rejuvenation. Ask Him to bless it with special times of communion with Him.

Think about what draws you to your favorite
room. Thank God for the gift of this space.

....

....

....

....

Gratitude for "No"

*For my thoughts are not your thoughts, nor are your
ways my ways, says the Lord. For as the heavens are
higher than the earth, so are my ways higher than
your ways and my thoughts than your thoughts.*

Isaiah 55:8–9 NRSV

If you tell a child "No" or "Not yet," that child doesn't say, "Okay. I know you're saying no out of love for me. I trust you're making the right decision." Imagine a three-year-old saying that as you take a five-pound bag of candy out of her hands and place it back on the store shelf. The response typically includes crying, pouting, and frustration. As the adult you know "No" is for the child's benefit. A parent's withholding is not to hurt, but to protect, because of deep love and care for his or her children.

When God tells you "No" or "Not yet," it hurts. You feel confused and frustrated, and you cry, mope, and yell. Do you believe God withholds *because* of His deep love for you? Even while it stings and you don't understand, you can be thankful for His all-knowing wisdom; His is a purposeful, loving, and protective "No." Give thanks for each *no* on your life journey. Rejoice in the Lord's plans for you. There's a divine purpose behind His *no*, and an even greater *yes* is ahead.

Think about the noes God has given or is presently giving you. Ask Him to reveal His good and loving character to you through His answer.

....

....

....

Boycotting the Blues

*No, in all these things we are more than
conquerors through him who loved us.*

ROMANS 8:37

Have you experienced the Sunday night blues? Many of us, even those of us who love our jobs, are familiar with this sinking feeling on Sunday afternoon or evening. The reality of another week is looming. Tomorrow might bring emails upon emails and dress pants instead of sweatpants or long days alone with your young kids.

The Sunday night blues tend to snuff out the fun you had during the weekend. As you prepare for another pressure-filled week, the blues focus on everything you didn't do: weeding, washing the car, organizing that darn closet, grocery shopping, quality time with your spouse. *All I want is another weekend*, you grumble.

What if you could end the weekend well? It begins with purposeful gratitude. What *did* you do? Perhaps you hiked, grabbed dinner with a friend, or watched your child's hockey game. Maybe you heard a great sermon. As you focus on the weekend's gifts, you'll feel more joyful and less disheartened; those memories and good things can carry you through the week. Boycott the Sunday night blues by recalling the weekend's wonders.

Find purposeful gratitude in what you did yesterday.

....

....

....

The East and the West

He has taken our sins away from us
as far as the east is from west.

PSALM 103:12 NCV

Psalm 103 says that when God forgives us, He removes our sins "as far as the east is from the west" (v. 12). You're probably thinking that's a significant distance, and it is! However, God's forgiveness is a gift even vaster and deeper than we understand. When traveling west, you will never hit an "end point." And when traveling east, you'll continue forever. His forgiveness is infinite, just as the east is from the west.

God's forgiveness is bigger than we can imagine. How does that make you feel?

....

....

....

....

....

....

Day 65

"Thank You for Hearing Me"

So they took away the stone. Then Jesus looked up and said, "Father, I thank you that you have heard me."

ather, thank you for hearing me. Jesus prayed these words outside His friend Lazarus's tomb. Jesus looked to the heavens and praised God for hearing His prayer before Lazarus had even come out of the tomb. What faith, to thank God for hearing Him even before the prayer had been answered. When you pray, thank God boldly for hearing you; Jesus' example shows we can believe the Lord hears our petitions—both spoken and in our hearts. Hallelujah!

Thank the Lord for always hearing your prayers. Ask Him to give you faith He will answer them.

....

....

....

....

....

The Blessings Dry Chicken Brings

Give praise to the Lord, proclaim his name; make known among the nations what he has done.

PSALM 105:1

Have you recently sat down to dinner and thought, *This meal again?* Maybe it's leftover soup for the third night in a row or you're at your mother-in-law's, eating her notoriously bland chicken casserole. You know every meal is a gift, but how can you be authentically grateful for mushy vegetable soup or dry chicken?

If you feel your heart sink as you look at the food in front of you, challenge yourself to be grateful in a different way. Look at everything on and around the table and give thanks. The salt shaker will come in handy with the chicken, the ice water is clean and drinkable, and you may not love the main course, but you love your mother-in-law. You're able to have fulfilling conversation with people you love, the leftover soup helped your grocery bill, and even the presence of the meal, tasteless as it may be, is a blessing. It nourishes your physical body, which, in turn, nourishes your mind.

There are blessings, big and small, on and around your dinner table. Look for these gifts the next time you pull out your chair.

Do you have "dry chicken" in your life? Look around it; what can you be grateful for?

....

....

....

....

....

Every meal is a gift.

The First Amendment

Christ made us free. So stand strong.
GALATIANS 5:1 NCV

Freedom of religion is one of our country's great values. We are free to choose the faith we cling to; we are not forced into worshipping a certain god. We can read our Bible on the subway without fear, attend a worship service of our choice, and speak about our faith without censoring.

In the Old Testament Daniel was thrown into the lion's den because he refused to bow to the king and continued praying even though a decree against his actions had been published. You might feel awkward when you bow your head to pray at a restaurant or hesitant about expressing your faith because of what others might think, but safety isn't an issue. You don't worry about confinement, labor camp, torture, and other repercussions.

A Pew Research study found that 75 percent of the world has severe religious restrictions, and the U.S. Department of State reports fellow believers in more than sixty countries face persecution from their government or fellow citizens.[1] Oh, how blessed we are to have freedom of religion!

List a few ways the First Amendment impacts your week.

Don't Let Comparison Steal from You

Devote yourselves to prayer, being watchful and thankful.
COLOSSIANS 4:2

You love your house . . . until you see one that's bigger, newer, and just . . . better. Stand on your guard; comparison is the thief of gratitude. It has power to snatch thankfulness from you in milliseconds. Take heart: you have a safeguard. If you place gratitude right in front of you, and you're alert to any predators, comparison and dissatisfaction cannot sneak in. They have no choice but to leave.

Are there specific comparisons you struggle with?

....

....

....

Day 69

The Blessing of
a Flat Tire

*Blessed be God—he heard me praying. He proved he's on
my side; I've thrown my lot in with him. Now I'm jumping
for joy, and shouting and singing my thanks to him.*
PSALM 28:6—7 MSG

Over the past few days, were you driving a vehicle,
riding a bus, hailing a cab, flying on a plane, catch-
ing a train, or utilizing the subway? Transportation is
so integrated into our lives that we rarely view it as a
gift. It affects our work, social life, and family, but we
don't notice our dependence on it until issues come up,
like getting a flat tire. Transportation is a gift; thank
God for the crowded subways, warm airplanes, and
Cheerio-strewn cars!

What type of transportation do you use? Turn a
few of your complaints about it into praises.

....

....

....

....

Day 70

The Colors of
the Rainbow

*At once I was in the Spirit, and there before me was a
throne in heaven with someone sitting on it. And the one
who sat there had the appearance of jasper and ruby. A
rainbow that shone like an emerald encircled the throne.*

REVELATION 4:2–3

The first color television was sold in the early 1950s
and began making its way into the living rooms of
Americans. What an experience it must have been for
viewers—to see vibrant colors on television after only
knowing pictures to be black and white.

It's hard to imagine our present visual entertainment in black and white. Color makes today's television
shows or movies more lively and interesting. Without
color it would feel like a different experience.

If color is that imperative in video entertainment,
imagine what our entire world would be like without
color. There would be no orange tiger lilies, deep pink
watermelon, or brilliantly blue seas. Everything would
be various shades of gray. We would miss the expanse
of an emerald forest or the captivating beauty of a male
peacock, and it would be difficult to see rainbows.
Could they even exist? Praise our Maker for forming
a world full of color. Notice the beauty of color in your
surroundings today.

If you could choose one color to see, which would it be and why? Praise our creative God for our colorful and vibrant world!

....

....

....

....

Overcoming Obstacles

Teach me thy way, O Lord, and lead me in a
plain path, because of mine enemies.

PSALM 27:11 KJV

I want to be more thankful and complain less, but when ____ happens, it's hard to do! If you run into obstacles trying to live a life of gratitude, don't worry; it's normal. What obstacles prevent you from having a grateful heart? A fussy child, bad traffic, work stress, comparison, cloudy weather, too much time spent away from Scripture? Take heart and be strong—the Lord is on your side!

Today focus on one obstacle and make an extra effort to fight against it.

....

....

....

Day 72

The Enriching
Gift of Smell

*But thanks be to God, who always leads us as captives
in Christ's triumphal procession and uses us to spread
the aroma of the knowledge of him everywhere. For
we are to God the pleasing aroma of Christ.*

2 CORINTHIANS 2:14–15

Imagine waking up without the ability to smell. You can't smell coffee brewing or cinnamon rolls baking. The calming effect of lavender is now obsolete. Smell is highly linked with emotions and mood. Now the fresh box of crayons doesn't smell like anything, when normally, the scent reminds you of childhood. Since smell greatly contributes to a flavor's impact, you can't taste either. How often do you take your sense of smell for granted? Think of all the ways it enriches your life.

If you could only smell one scent for the rest of your life, what would it be?

....

....

....

....

Day 73

Make Music to the Lord

*Praise him with the sounding of the trumpet, praise him
with the harp and lyre, praise him with timbrel and
dancing, praise him with the strings and pipe, praise him
with the clash of cymbals, praise him with resounding
cymbals. Let everything that has breath praise the Lord.*

PSALM 150:3–6

Music is a powerful art. It intensifies movies, gets stuck in our heads, and propels us to action. Without it church would be very quiet, parades would be dull, exercise would lose a motivational tool, and many people would not sleep as well. Music aids literacy, draws people together, and benefits individuals with struggles such as autism, Alzheimer's disease, and substance abuse. It greatly affects our mental, physical, spiritual, and emotional well-being.

Scripture is jam-packed with references to music. The horn, lyre, bagpipe (NASB), trumpet, flute, tambourine (NLT), and cymbals are a few instruments mentioned. David's harp playing soothed and relaxed King Saul when an evil spirit troubled him. In the parable of the lost son, the father threw a party with music and dancing. Angels rejoiced at Jesus' birth. Moses and the Israelites sang after the Red Sea victory, and when the ark of the covenant was brought to the temple, musicians were accompanied by 120 trumpet-playing priests.

The Lord uses music in so many ways. Praise Him for creating this beautiful art form!

Is there a specific song you love singing to the Lord? Why?

....

....

....

Day 74

The Blessings
We Can't See

God doesn't take back the gifts he has given or forget
about the people he has chosen. . . . Who can measure
the wealth and wisdom and knowledge of God? Who
can understand his decisions or explain what he
does? "Has anyone known the thoughts of the Lord or
given him advice? Has anyone loaned something to
the Lord that must be repaid?" Everything comes from
the Lord. All things were made because of him and
will return to him. Praise the Lord forever! Amen.

ROMANS 11:29, 33–36 CEV

When we become part of God's family, He lavishes us with spiritual blessings. They aren't material—we can't see them—but they change our life now and for eternity.

There are far too many to name, but here are a few: God chose us, says Ephesians 2, "even when we were dead in sins" (v. 5 KJV). He rescues us with salvation and adopts us as His children. He lavishes us with grace and redemption, grants forgiveness from our sins, and calls us holy and blameless. The Lord sanctifies us, pours out unconditional love, provides the Holy Spirit's guidance, and frees us from sin's power. We have an eternal inheritance. "We are His heirs along with the Anointed, set to inherit everything that is

His" (Romans 8:17 THE VOICE). We have wisdom, peace, purpose, hope, and assurance that nothing can separate us from His love.

Our Father opens His arms wide, and we receive "every spiritual blessing in Christ" (Ephesians 1:3). He withholds nothing!

God gives us an inheritance of spiritual blessings. Choose to bless others with the spiritual blessings you're given. What are those blessings you see in your life now?

....

....

....

What's Your Response?

Bless our God, O peoples, let the sound of his
praise be heard, who has kept us among the
living, and has not let our feet slip.
PSALM 66:8–9 NRSV

You're running low on groceries. All you have are five loaves of bread and a couple of tilapia. Suddenly your doorbell rings. Five thousand people are outside; they hear you're providing lunch. How would you respond?

In the Bible story of feeding the five thousand, the disciples responded, "We have nothing here but five loaves and two fish" (Matthew 14:17 NRSV). Jesus responded with thankfulness to His Father. He didn't view the bread and fish as "nothing." He didn't fret. He gave thanks for what He had, and then He trusted God, and He fed them all.

How would you respond if five thousand people came to your door expecting lunch?

....

....

....

....

At the Forefront of Our Minds

*Give to the LORD the glory he deserves! Bring
your offering and come into his presence.
Worship the LORD in all his holy splendor.*

1 CHRONICLES 16:29 NLT

Have you heard the quote, "What if you wake up today with only the things you thanked God for yesterday?" What a question! It prompts us to put gratitude at the forefront of our minds. It's easy to dive into prayer with requests and concerns, but we also need to praise the Lord for His daily innumerable gifts. Maybe you only brought requests and questions before the Lord yesterday; He will always give you a chance to begin again. Be quick to thank our generous Giver today.

What did you thank God for yesterday? Be
mindful of thanking Him throughout the day!

....

....

....

....

More Than a Fill-in-the-Blank List

Lord, our Lord, how majestic is your name in all the earth!
PSALM 8:9

In Psalm 8 David praised God's glory, strength, creation, and love for humankind. But he didn't simply list those things; his gratitude was more than a fill-in-the-blank list. It was richer and deeper.

When David gave thanks for God's care for humans, it was not a bare-bones outline. In great detail he told how God shows His care for man: He crowns them with glory and honor; He charges man with authority. And David didn't simply say man is over "all things." He got specific, naming flocks, herds, animals, birds, fish, and everything in the ocean.

It's as if he couldn't fathom simply saying, "Thank you for _____." He knew God's goodness is more than a list. It's like a menu board saying the special is meat, potatoes, and vegetables. It's true, but there's more. The waitress raves over the special: "Tonight's dinner is smoked lamb shank braised in Italian red wine and rosemary, served over potato mousseline, with caramelized squash, asparagus tips, and locally harvested microgreens." She appreciates the meal and doesn't want to leave any detail out. When we thank God for His gifts, we need to remember the richness of His gifts and exuberantly give thanks. His blessings are much more than a generic list; they can't be contained in a few words. Let your mouth overflow with gratitude!

Do you pray "fill-in-the-blank" prayers? Try to add more detail and note how it makes you feel.

....

....

....

Day 78

Travel Near and Far

If I take the wings of the morning and settle at the farthest limits of the sea, even there your hand shall lead me, and your right hand shall hold me fast.

PSALM 139:9–10 NRSV

Travel is a privilege. If you studied abroad for a semester, went to Disneyland as a kid, camped the next county over, or lived as an expatriate, that new experience was a gift. The next time you travel, whether your destination is near or far, you lodge in a tent or an all-inclusive resort, or leave for a day or year, thank the Creator for the gift of experiencing new places in His beautiful world.

Where do you dream of traveling? Where have you already been?

....

....

....

....

....

Day 79

Sick, But Not Distressed

Yours, LORD, is the greatness and the power and
the glory and the majesty and the splendor, for
everything in heaven and earth is yours.

1 CHRONICLES 29:11

Your body is aching and feverish. You're coughing, exacerbating your sore throat. Yep, you're sick. It may not be convenient, but you aren't distressed. An urgent-care clinic is nearby. Your city has good hospitals, highly trained doctors and nurses, pharmacists, and health-care professionals. Proper sanitation is practiced, and drugstores are stocked with supplies. We don't know a life without these lifesaving gifts, and for that, we live in luxury.

What are other luxuries we have that others do not?

....

....

....

....

....

Day 80

The Strangers Working to Keep You Safe

Defend the poor and fatherless; do justice to the
afflicted and needy. Deliver the poor and needy;
free them from the hand of the wicked.
PSALM 82:3–4 NKJV

hildren often light up when they see a fire truck, police car, or ambulance. These vehicles make noise and travel fast. Though you may be less enthralled with the sirens and speed, you're certainly grateful to hear those sirens when you're in need. You know the people in the emergency vehicle (firefighters, police officers, EMTs, first responders) are there to help. They are working to keep you safe. It's their duty to help, support, and protect the people in your community.

Have you ever stopped to thank someone who works to keep you safe? There are more than we realize! It could be someone in public safety, the military, a medical staff member, an emergency dispatcher, a criminal investigator, or a security guard. Many of these jobs involve some risk, and often, these individuals are manning life-threatening situations: forest fires, collapsing buildings, or high-risk criminals. They work to keep you safe though you may be a perfect stranger, and they put their lives in danger for you every day. What a gift!

Choose one type of "stranger" and thank God for all that person does.

....

....

....

Am I Rich?

God is able to bless you abundantly, so that
in all things at all times, having all that you
need, you will abound in every good work.

2 CORINTHIANS 9:8

*R*ich is relative. In a study by UBS Investor Relations, four in ten Americans with assets of five million dollars or more don't consider themselves rich.[1] If that five million were a salary, your monthly paycheck would be approximately four hundred thousand dollars. That monthly wage is more than the average American household brings in per year. So it's all relative.

Whether you make twenty million or twenty thousand, you're wealthy compared to much of the world. Even if you struggle to pay your bills, are eating rice and beans again, and rely on food stamps and government assistance; even if your car struggles to complete your daily commute—even then, you are fortunate.

Many in our world don't have the bare necessities: food, clean water, clothing, or a home. Their very existence is a struggle. In the United States clean drinking water is everywhere: in supermarkets, airports, parks, restaurants, libraries, schools. Though our system is not perfect, soup kitchens and food pantries, shelters, public housing, job training, and free education are available. Brother, sister, let gratitude fill your heart as you contemplate the wealth you have. We are all rich indeed.

How does the above make you feel about being rich?

....

....

....

....

The Sweetest Sleep

Stay calm; there is no need to be afraid of a sudden disaster or to worry when calamity strikes the wicked, for the Eternal is always there to protect you. He will safeguard your each and every step.

PROVERBS 3:25–26 THE VOICE

Are you a night worrier? Do you have trouble sleeping? Be comforted. God gifts us with a remedy for long and sleepless nights. Proverbs 3 says God gives wisdom and knowledge to steer us so we "will not trip *or fall*" (v. 23 THE VOICE). How freeing! Our minds will be "*clear*, free from fear," and "when you lie down *to rest*, you will *be refreshed by* sweet sleep" (v. 24). With our Father's wisdom and knowledge and with trust in His protection, we can enjoy sweet sleep.

God is your great protector. How can that truth give you sweet sleep tonight?

....

....

....

....

....

Lost and Found

Then she will call in her friends and neighbors
and say, "Let's celebrate! I've found the coin I lost."
Jesus said, "In the same way God's angels are
happy when even one person turns to him."
LUKE 15:9–10 CEV

Everywhere. *I've looked everywhere*, you think. Have you ever lost something personally valuable? You search every crevice and corner. You refuse to give up because you've lost something precious. Beloved, this is how the Lord sees you: you are irreplaceable, valuable, and worth every second of His time. He will tirelessly pursue you. We serve a God who never quits on us—His persistence is a gift, and His joy when He finds His lost child is unmatchable. Praise our Father, who never ever gives up on us.

Describe the feelings and emotions of finding something that's lost. Do you believe God feels that deep joy about you?

....

....

....

....

Day 84

The Double Meaning of *Why Me?*

O sing to the LORD a new song, for He has done
wonderful things, His right hand and His holy
arm have gained the victory for Him.
PSALM 98:1 NASB

The question *Why me?* can be interpreted two ways. Is it surprised and amazed? Or does it sound more like anguish? There's a song by country singer Kris Kristofferson titled "Why Me," and it sold more than one million records, becoming the biggest hit in his music career. By the title alone you'd think he's asking the question begrudgingly. But the lyrics go on to reveal deep humility and gratitude by asking, instead, why he deserves all the blessings he's known in life.

The next time you open your mouth to ask *Why me?*, will it be in praise of the Father? When you shift your words and mind-set to a *Why me?* of joy and astonishment, you immerse yourself in appreciation. This doesn't mean you should *fake it till you make it* when conversing with the Lord; He can handle your distressed and confused *Why me?* But if you find yourself continually asking this question with self-pity and an attitude of entitlement, pause to consider your heart, dear friend. May our hearts be constantly searching for a path toward thankfulness to our Savior.

Try taking the mind-set of surprise and gratitude when you think, Why me? What gifts come to mind?

....

....

....

The Gift Only the Elderly Can Give

Is not wisdom found among the aged? Does not long life bring understanding?

JOB 12:12

When you hear the word *elderly*, what comes to mind? Frail and needy? Sage and essential? Do you view older people as gifts?

Rich experience and knowledge can only come with age. Older women in Hawaii teach younger generations the art of crafting leis. Aboriginal Australians look to elders for cultural knowledge, decision-making, and leadership abilities. The elderly in the United States underwent tragic events, like the Great Depression, the Vietnam War, and JFK's assassination. They survived unimaginable things, and their struggles and victories can enlighten and teach us.

In studies, their frequent advice focuses on appreciating the present. They advise: The way you start your day really matters. Don't let money be your number one priority. Stop worrying, and don't worry about things out of your control—they may never happen. Find and follow your passions. Work a job you enjoy. Learn to savor simple pleasures. Happiness is a choice.

That advice is valuable, and the elderly's life experience and knowledge are gifts no one else can give.

Do you have anyone elderly in your life? What have you learned from them?

....

....

....

The ABCs of Gratitude

Out of his fullness we have all received
grace in place of grace already given.

JOHN 1:16

Did you ever have writer's block in school—you racked your brain, but the page stayed blank? We can also experience this with gratitude. Let's call it *gratitude block*. Your mind is blanking on the gifts in your life. Go back to the basics and think of the alphabet. Try listing gifts from A to Z, or focus on one specific letter. *A* = adventure, acceptance, or adoption. The more you practice gratitude, the easier it gets—just like the ABCs.

Write out a gratitude list from A to Z.

....

....

....

....

....

Honesty
is a gift

Unflinching Honesty

In the same way that iron sharpens iron, a
person sharpens the character of his friend.
PROVERBS 27:17 THE VOICE

A re there friends in your life who give you unflinching honesty? Honesty strengthens integrity, shows
you care, and gives you freedom, but it doesn't always
feel good. It can make us flinch, get nervous, feel
embarrassed or even defensive. It might be pain-
ful or uncomfortable. But in the end honesty is a gift
that sharpens us and others, teaches our hearts to be
humble, and keeps our character strong.

Have you ever been the bearer, or receiver, of
unflinching honesty? What good came out of it?

....

....

....

....

....

....

Day 88

Uncovering Gifts with Our Senses

I will give thanks to you, LORD, with all my heart; I will tell of all your wonderful deeds. I will be glad and rejoice in you; I will sing the praises of your name, O Most High.

PSALM 9:1–2

Babies use their developing senses of sight, sound, smell, taste, and touch to explore and understand their environment. They are curious little humans, ready to soak everything up. If there's a cardboard box on the floor, babies don't overlook it. To them it's a new toy. They look at the box from all angles, bang it on the floor, try to eat it, sniff it, and feel the cardboard texture beneath their chubby fingers.

If *we* saw a cardboard box on the floor, we would barely notice it. It's just a box . . . or is it?

When you *see* the box, it may remind you of what it held: a window air conditioner to help cool off your humid house. When you *hear* the box being banged on the floor, you may appreciate that it's keeping your child occupied so you can have a few minutes of peace. Do you see how, when activating your senses, you uncover gifts even if they aren't obvious at first glance? God's gifts are all around—even in the form of a cardboard box.

Use your senses to uncover God's gifts right now.
What are they?

....

....

....

....

....

....

....

Beyond Prayer and Praise

Therefore, since we are receiving a kingdom that cannot be shaken, let us be thankful, and so worship God acceptably with reverence and awe.

HEBREWS 12:28

Prayer and singing are powerful ways to worship, but they aren't the only means. Psalm 9:11 says, "Tell among the peoples his deeds!" (ESV). We show gratitude by telling others about Jesus. We praise Him through loving all people He's created—even the most unlovable. We obey His commands with joy, serve others as Jesus did, and forgive others. Use your talents, take good care of His creation, and study His words, keeping them close to your heart. Go beyond prayer and praise.

How are you most comfortable thanking God? How can you praise Him in new ways?

....

....

....

....

Day 90

Education's Accessibility

Hold on to instruction, do not let it go;
guard it well, for it is your life.

PROVERBS 4:13

Packing lunches, school bus rides, homework, new teachers—does this sound familiar? The ability to go to school seems normal to us. Yet easy accessibility to education is a gift. In the beginning of the twentieth century, average American children attended school for only a few years. Many schools closed during the Great Depression. Segregated schools weren't fully eliminated until the late 1970s, and in 1980, the number of women in college finally became equal to men. Education's quality and accessibility has come so far. Without it you likely wouldn't be reading these words!

What are three ways education has benefited you?

....

....

....

....

....

Day 91

Mary's Song

She spoke out with a loud voice and said, "Blessed are you
among women, and blessed is the fruit of your womb!"

LUKE 1:42 NKJV

In Luke 1 the angel Gabriel appeared to Mary and commanded her: "Rejoice" (v. 28 CEB). Before he even told her why he was there, he urged Mary to give thanks, for he knew he was bringing good news—the best news, in fact. After she recovered from the shock of having an angel in her home, as well as learning she would bear the Savior of the world, Mary responded with rejoicing.

This was shocking, glorious, life-changing news that would impact the world forever. It was complicated and more than a little mysterious. Instead of worrying, Mary chose to trust the Lord and gave thanks with heartfelt sincerity. "And Mary said: 'My soul magnifies the Lord, and my spirit has rejoiced in God my Savior. . . . For He who is mighty has done great things for me, and holy is His name'" (Luke 1:46–47, 49 NKJV). Mary's beautiful prayer of gratitude is an example of giving thanks, not because she had it all figured out—she was a virgin, yet she was pregnant?—but because she trusted the Father and His goodness.

Beloved, regardless of your circumstance and even in your confusion, thank your heavenly Father for who He is. May gratitude constantly spill from your heart, mouth, and life.

How would you have reacted in Mary's position?

....

....

....

Day 92

Circumstances Change, but God Never Does

But You are the same, and Your years will have no end.

PSALM 102:27 NKJV

The Greek philosopher Heraclitus said, "The only thing constant is change." We change physically, spiritually, emotionally, and cognitively our entire lives. The weather changes daily. It seems a teenager's mood changes minute by minute. Technology, situations, seasons, relationships, tides—they are ever changing and shifting.

The philosopher was correct. Change in our world is constant. But believers have a surety in Someone constant: our God never changes, and neither does His Word. He is the same yesterday, today, and tomorrow, through the end of time, and He will never break His promises. Hebrews 1:10–12 says, "In the beginning, Lord, you laid the foundations of the earth, and the heavens are the work of your hands. They will perish, but you remain; they will all wear out like a garment. You will roll them up like a robe; like a garment they will be changed. But you remain the same, and your years will never end." Repeat that to yourself: *You remain the same, and your years will never end.* Thanks be to our immutable King!

Over the past year what has changed in your life?

....

....

....

What Epidemic Will You Spread?

Your words were found and I ate them, and Your words
became for me a joy and the delight of my heart; for I
have been called by Your name, O LORD God of hosts.
JEREMIAH 15:16 NASB

Your actions, emotions, and words are contagious. If you show appreciation to your employees, they will feel valued. Because of your kind words, they will return home and speak lovingly to their spouses. They'll vocalize their appreciation for a home-cooked meal. This positive exchange will benefit the kids, and they'll, in turn, bring that gratitude into their classrooms, where it will be spread to even more families. Gratitude breeds gratitude, but it needs to start with someone. An epidemic of gratitude begins with you.

How can you begin spreading the epidemic of gratitude?

....

....

....

....

Day 94

Reading, the Limitless Gift

*Let us come into his presence with thanksgiving; let
us make a joyful noise to him with songs of praise! For
the LORD is a great God, and a great King above all gods.*

PSALM 95:2–3 NRSV

We read constantly: emails and Facebook updates, nutrition labels, advertisements, and notes. Reading informs us of current events, educates on specific topics, and broadens our perspective. It's a gift we use constantly yet barely notice. It's a usable and entertaining skill for anyone. Reading exercises our brains and teaches new facts and vocabulary. Board books, chapter books, classics, Pulitzer Prize winners, and magazine articles have power to transport and transform; we can experience a faraway land, become a superhero, learn a craft, deepen our spiritual life, examine God's words, or study historical accounts. Reading is a limitless gift!

What is the most impactful book, article, or quote you've read?

....

....

....

Day 95

The Women

She is clothed with strength and dignity;
she can laugh at the days to come.

PROVERBS 31:25

Courageous, strong, remarkable women have impacted history in major ways. Thank the Lord for women like Harriet Tubman, Anne Frank, and Rosa Parks. If we go back even further to biblical times, we find several influential and inspirational women to be grateful for. Deborah was a prophetess, the fifth judge raised up by God, and a military leader. Rahab hid spies on her roof, putting her life at risk, but in the long run, saving Israel. Mary, the mother of Jesus, was humble and obedient, quick to praise the Lord. Ruth was extremely loyal, ultimately becoming part of the line of Jesus. Esther put her marriage and life in danger by boldly coming before King Ahasuerus, her husband, for the sake of her people. Tabitha served the poor and made clothing for widows.

Our God gave them each specific talents and callings. Each one lived a unique story, and each one impacted history in her own way. Praise the Lord for these women who were faithful, obedient, and powerfully used in His perfect purpose and plan.

Name influential women in your life. What have you learned from them? How do they inspire you?

He Chooses the Unqualified

Remember what you were when God chose you.
. . . God chose the foolish things of this world to
put the wise to shame. He chose the weak things
of this world to put the powerful to shame.

1 CORINTHIANS 1:26–27 CEV

Our God is not partial; His gifts are for everyone, not reserved for the wealthiest or the most popular, beautiful, powerful, or talented. He picks flawed sinners and everyday commoners to spread His truth. He chose Mary, a young virgin, to birth the Savior of the world. He used Moses, a self-proclaimed non-eloquent speaker, to lead the Israelites. God selected Rahab, a prostitute; Abraham, an elderly man; David, an adulterer and murderer. He sent the Savior as a baby, used a young boy to kill Goliath, and His disciples were ordinary, blue-collar individuals. He uses people like you and like me. Worship our gracious and just God for using ordinary people for extraordinarily divine purposes.

Do you believe God can use you and your weaknesses in mighty ways?

....

....

His *gifts* are for
everyone

Day 97

Grace, Not Perfection

*Christ gave each one of us the special gift of
grace, showing how generous he is.*
EPHESIANS 4:7 NCV

In 1726 Benjamin Franklin created an organized system for attaining moral perfection. He sought to achieve thirteen virtues, such as temperance, order, frugality, sincerity, justice, cleanliness, and humility. Though his plan was well thought-out, Franklin was never able to achieve perfection. Our Father knows, despite our best efforts, that we can't either. Be filled with joy because our imperfections are covered by Jesus, so God sees us through grace-filled eyes. Grace, not perfection, is the song of our lives!

Praise God for His grace!

....

....

....

....

....

....

God sees us through grace-filled eyes

Day 98

Soak Up the Season

He changes the times and the seasons; He removes
kings and raises up kings; He gives wisdom to the wise
and knowledge to those who have understanding.

DANIEL 2:21 NKJV

Seasons have a beginning and an end. They either feel endless or not long enough, and not everyone is satisfied with the current season. When it's summer, we begin yearning for fall's pumpkin patches and cider. We pray for spring while shoveling the snow from our driveways. And while we're busy wishing one season away, we're missing the beauty of the present.

Isn't life a lot like the seasons? When we're in high school, we want to be in college. When we're single, we want to be married. When we're married, we want kids. When we have children, we want more freedom. When we are unemployed, we want a job. When we have a job, we want more vacation time. And so on.

Soak up the season you're in. You can't rush a season, and if you only yearn for a change, you'll overlook the raw beauty currently surrounding you. Sometimes change is near, but it's hidden in the thawing earth or in the skies, waiting for its time. Thank God for the present season, and praise Him for reigning over all our life's seasons.

Don't miss the beauty of the current season of life in which you find yourself. What are the good things about this period of time?

....

....

....

Day 99

On Forgiveness

*Let all bitterness and wrath and anger and clamor
and slander be put away from you, along with all
malice. Be kind to one another, tenderhearted, forgiving
one another, as God in Christ forgave you.*
EPHESIANS 4:31–32 ESV

You feel anger, bitterness, resentment, and revenge when someone hurts you. You don't want to forgive. How can you, when you feel so angry? Friend, forgiveness is a choice to give an undeserved gift. It's also a gift to yourself; you will feel emotional and physical blessings when you decide to forgive. Experiments at the University of Washington discovered unforgiveness literally weighs a person down.[1] Studies also show those who forgive have better physical health, higher self-esteem, and healthier relationships.[2]

Forgiveness is tough. But it's also liberating. With it you can be freed from the past and relieved of your burden. Because Jesus has lavished us with the gift of undeserved forgiveness, we, too, can offer the gift of forgiveness to others. Colossians 3 says, "Bear with each other and forgive one another if any of you has a grievance against someone. Forgive as the Lord forgave you" (v. 13). Are you staggering under a burden of bitterness? Throw it off. Be released. Usher in gratitude for the ability to be forgiven and to forgive. Let your soul rejoice in the freedom forgiveness brings.

How has forgiveness (either from God or another person) positively impacted you?

....

....

....

Old Words, Powerful Message

The fruit of the Spirit is love, joy, peace,
forbearance, kindness, goodness, faithfulness,
gentleness and self-control.

GALATIANS 5:22—23

Marcus Tullius Cicero, known as Rome's greatest orator, died in 43 BC, but his words have relevance today: "Gratitude is not only the greatest of virtues, but the parent of all others." Can you see the truth in this quote? When grateful, we become patient, not restless; we have peace, not anxiety. We choose generosity over selfishness, joy over resentment, worship over complaining. Temperance replaces excess; mistakes become lessons; lack becomes abundance. Our entire perspective changes.

When you choose gratitude, how does it affect you spiritually, emotionally, and physically?

....

....

....

....

When *grateful*,
we become **patient**

Notes

Introduction

1. Wayne Martindale and Jerry Root, eds., *The Quotable Lewis* (Wheaton, IL: Tyndale House Publishers, 1990), 579.

Day 5: 7.6 Billion

1. "World Population Clock: 7.6 Billion People (2017)," Worldometers, http://www.worldometers.info/world-population/.

Day 67: The First Amendment

1. Open Doors USA, Christian Persecution, Open Doors, accessed November 21, 2017, https://www.opendoorsusa.org/christian-persecution/.

Chapter 81: Am I Rich?

1. Brad Tuttle, "What It Means to Be 'Wealthy' in America Today," *TIME*, July 24, 2013, http://business.time.com/2013/07/24/what-it-means-to-be-wealthy-in-america-today/.

Day 99: On Forgiveness

1. Olga Khazan, "The Forgiveness Boost," *The Atlantic*, January 28, 2015, https://www.theatlantic.com/health/archive/2015/01/the-forgiveness-boost/384796/.

2. Everett L. Worthington Jr., "The New Science of Forgiveness," *Greater Good Magazine*, September 1, 2004, https://greatergood.berkeley.edu/article/item/the_new_science_of_forgiveness.